MEL ROBBINS

Let Them Theory Book

Pioneering Personal Development for Generations to Come

Charley C. Goff

Copyright © 2025 by Charley C. Goff

All rights reserved. No part of this book may be reproduced, distributed, or transmitted in any form or by any means, including photocopying, recording, or other electronic or mechanical methods.
Without the publisher's prior written permission, except for brief quotations embodied in critical reviews and certain noncommercial uses permitted by copyright law.

MANUFACTURED IN UNITED STATES OF AMERICA

CONTENTS

INTRODUCTION	5
THE ACADEMIC AND CAREER LABYRINTH	13
THE RIPPLE EFFECT OF INFLUENCE	21
EMPOWERING THE MASSES THROUGH ACTIONABLE WISDOM	35
EMBRACING THE FUTURE WITH CONFIDENCE AND COURAGE	43
BECOMING A GLOBAL VOICE FOR CHANGE	52
CONCLUSION	60

Introduction

Mel Robbins—a name that resonates with resilience, reinvention, and relentless pursuit of change. To understand the sheer magnitude of her impact on millions across the globe, one must first unravel the tapestry of her life. It is a story stitched with threads of triumph and tribulation, colored by moments of despair and redemption, and ultimately bound together by a remarkable ability to transform personal struggles into universal inspiration. Hers is not merely the tale of a successful author or a celebrated speaker; it is the chronicle of a woman who dared to defy convention, embraced vulnerability, and ignited a movement that reshaped the contours of modern self-help culture.

From the very beginning, Mel's life was marked by paradoxes. Born into a middle-class family in a small New England town, she was surrounded by the quintessential markers of suburban stability. Yet, beneath the surface of this apparent normalcy lay a young girl grappling with self-doubt and an insatiable yearning to carve out a space for herself in the world. Her childhood was a delicate dance between expectation and aspiration, a balancing act that would later define much of her adult life. While her peers navigated the predictable paths of adolescence, Mel was already questioning the rules, seeking answers to questions most hadn't yet thought to ask. What does it mean to succeed? Why does failure sting so sharply? And perhaps most importantly, how does one find the courage to stand tall when the weight of the world seems insurmountable?

Education was both an anchor and a battlefield for Mel. Academically inclined but socially uncertain, she often found herself teetering on the edge of self-imposed isolation. Her teachers saw potential; her classmates saw an enigma. But Mel saw herself as something entirely different: a work in progress. It was during these formative years that she began to develop a profound sense of empathy—a quality that would later become the cornerstone of her connection with audiences worldwide. She learned to listen, to observe, to understand the silent struggles that others carried. And in doing so, she began to recognize her own resilience, a quiet strength that would one day roar loudly enough to shake the foundations of complacency in countless lives.

The transition from high school to college marked the beginning of Mel's foray into the complexities of adult life. She pursued a degree in law, a field that promised prestige and stability but offered little in the way of passion or purpose. Yet, as she immersed herself in the rigorous demands of legal studies, she discovered a latent talent for persuasion and advocacy. The courtroom, she realized, was not merely a place for legal arguments; it was a stage for storytelling, a platform where narratives could shape destinies. This realization planted the seeds of a lifelong fascination with the power of words—their ability to inspire, to heal, and to transform.

But the glittering promise of a legal career soon gave way to the harsh realities of professional life. Mel's early years as a lawyer were marked by an unrelenting pressure to conform, to succeed within the rigid confines of a system that left little room for creativity or individuality. The long hours and high stakes took their toll, eroding her sense of self and leaving her questioning the very path she had chosen. By the time she reached her early thirties, Mel found herself at a crossroads, grappling with the dissonance between her outward achievements and her inner dissatisfaction. It was a period of profound disillusionment, a dark night of the soul that would ultimately serve as the crucible for her transformation.

The turning point came not with a grand epiphany but with a series of small, seemingly inconsequential decisions. At a time when her marriage was strained, her finances were in disarray, and her self-esteem was at an all-time low, Mel stumbled upon a deceptively simple idea that would change the trajectory of her life. The 5 Second

Rule—a mechanism as unassuming as it was revolutionary. It began as a personal experiment, a way to silence the self-sabotaging voices in her head and propel herself into action. But what started as a private coping strategy soon revealed itself to be a universal tool, one capable of dismantling the barriers of procrastination, fear, and self-doubt that plague so many.

Mel's journey from personal crisis to global influence was anything but linear. It was a path fraught with setbacks and self-doubt, punctuated by moments of clarity and courage. As she began to share her insights with others, first through small speaking engagements and later through larger platforms, she discovered the profound impact of her message. People from all walks of life—students, professionals, parents, and entrepreneurs—found solace and strength in her words. They saw in her a reflection of their own struggles and a beacon of hope for their own potential.

What sets Mel apart from many of her contemporaries is her unwavering authenticity. She does not present herself as a guru or a savior but as a fellow traveler on the journey of self-discovery. Her candor about her own imperfections, her willingness to share the messy, unvarnished truth of her experiences, has endeared her to millions. Whether standing on a stage before thousands or speaking directly into a camera for her social media followers, Mel exudes a rare combination of relatability and authority. She is at once a trusted guide and a relatable friend, someone who has walked the path she now illuminates for others.

As her influence grew, so too did her vision. Mel's work transcended the confines of motivational speaking and self-help literature, evolving into a broader mission to empower individuals to take control of their lives. Her books, *The 5 Second Rule* and *The High 5 Habit*, are not merely manuals for personal growth; they are invitations to embrace courage, to celebrate oneself, and to act with intention. Through these works, Mel has not only inspired change but has also created a framework for sustaining it, offering practical tools and strategies that resonate across cultures and contexts.

The legacy of Mel Robbins is not measured in accolades or sales figures but in the lives she has touched. It is evident in the testimonials of those who credit her with helping them overcome crippling anxiety, launch new careers, or rebuild broken relationships. It is reflected in the ripple effects of her teachings, as individuals empowered by her message go on to inspire change in their own communities. And it is embodied in the countless moments of action and courage that her work has sparked—moments that might otherwise have been lost to hesitation or fear.

Mel Robbins is, above all, a testament to the power of reinvention. Her story is a reminder that failure is not a final destination but a stepping stone to greater possibilities. It is an invitation to embrace the messy, imperfect process of growth and to recognize that within each of us lies the capacity for extraordinary transformation. As we delve deeper into the chapters of her life, we uncover not just the story of one woman's journey but a roadmap for our own. It is a journey that challenges us to break the mold, to defy the limits we place on ourselves, and to step boldly into the life we are meant to live.

Chapter: 01

The Academic and Career Labyrinth

Mel Robbins' journey through academia and the early years of her career is a story of ambition, disillusionment, and eventual awakening. It is a period that reveals the depth of her determination, the complexity of her character, and the foundation upon which she would later build her transformative impact. To fully appreciate the wisdom she imparts today, one must first understand the challenges and choices that shaped her during these formative years. These were the years when Mel's grit was tested, her identity was questioned, and her path seemed shrouded in uncertainty.

Her decision to pursue a legal career was emblematic of a time when societal expectations often dictated personal aspirations. Law promised prestige, financial security, and a clear trajectory of success. For Mel, it seemed like a logical choice, a way to prove her worth in a world that often equated value with titles and achievements. Yet, from the moment she stepped into her first lecture hall, she felt an inexplicable unease. The material was intellectually stimulating, but the environment felt stifling. It was as though she were wearing a suit tailored for someone else, restrictive and ill-fitting.

Nevertheless, Mel threw herself into her studies with characteristic fervor. Her professors recognized her as a diligent and capable student, one who was not afraid to challenge conventional wisdom or explore alternative perspectives. She excelled academically, mastering the intricacies of legal theory and honing her skills in argumentation and critical thinking. But beneath the accolades and accomplishments, a quiet discontent began to simmer. She often found herself questioning the very foundations of the legal system she was being trained to uphold. Why did justice so often seem elusive? Why were the voices of the marginalized and the vulnerable drowned out by the machinery of bureaucracy and power?

These questions lingered in the back of her mind as she graduated and entered the workforce. The transition from student to professional was both exhilarating and daunting. Mel secured a position at a prestigious law firm, a milestone that marked the culmination of years of hard work. Yet, the reality of practicing law soon collided with her expectations. The long hours, the high-pressure environment, and the cutthroat competition left little room for creativity or individuality. She found herself navigating a world where success was measured not by the impact one made but by the hours billed and the cases won.

Her disillusionment deepened as she witnessed the ethical compromises and systemic inequalities that permeated the legal profession. She began to feel like a cog in a machine, her individuality subsumed by the relentless demands of her job. The sense of purpose that had once driven her began to erode, replaced by a growing sense of alienation. She found herself questioning not only her career choice but also the broader societal values that had led her to this point. What did it mean to lead a meaningful life? Was success worth the sacrifice of one's authenticity and well-being?

The strain of her professional life began to seep into her personal relationships. Mel's marriage to her husband, Christopher Robbins, faced significant challenges during this period. The couple grappled with financial instability, communication breakdowns, and the stress of balancing career aspirations with family responsibilities. It was a time of profound uncertainty, marked by moments of despair and self-doubt. Yet, even in the midst of these struggles, Mel's resilience and resourcefulness shone through. She refused to succumb to despair, instead channeling her energy into finding solutions and seeking clarity.

It was during this tumultuous period that Mel began to explore alternative avenues of self-expression and fulfillment. She took on freelance writing projects, delving into topics that piqued her curiosity and allowed her to connect with others on a more personal level. Writing became a refuge, a way for her to process her experiences and articulate her thoughts. It was through this creative outlet that she began to rediscover her voice and reconnect with her passions. The act of putting pen to paper, of distilling complex emotions into words, was both cathartic and empowering.

At the same time, Mel began to immerse herself in the burgeoning field of personal development. She devoured books, attended seminars, and sought out mentors who could provide guidance and inspiration. She was particularly drawn to the work of thought leaders who emphasized the importance of mindset, resilience, and intentional action. Their teachings resonated deeply with her, sparking a sense of curiosity and possibility that had long been dormant. She began to see her struggles not as insurmountable obstacles but as opportunities for growth and transformation.

The turning point came when Mel decided to leave her legal career behind. It was a decision fraught with uncertainty, one that defied conventional wisdom and carried significant financial and emotional risks. Yet, for Mel, it was a necessary step toward reclaiming her authenticity and aligning her life with her values. She understood that true fulfillment could not be found within the confines of a career that stifled her creativity and compromised her integrity. With courage and conviction, she embarked on a new path, one that would ultimately lead her to become a beacon of hope and empowerment for others.

Mel's early forays into the world of personal development were marked by a relentless pursuit of knowledge and a deep commitment to self-improvement. She experimented with various techniques and strategies, refining her approach through trial and error. She also began to share her insights with others, initially through small workshops and speaking engagements. Her authenticity and relatability quickly set her apart, drawing audiences who were hungry for practical tools and genuine connection. Mel's ability to distill complex concepts into actionable steps, combined with her candid storytelling, made her a compelling and relatable presence.

As her reputation grew, so too did her platform. Mel's work began to gain traction, resonating with individuals from diverse backgrounds and walks of life. She was particularly attuned to the struggles of those who felt stuck, overwhelmed, or uncertain about their next steps. Her message was simple yet profound: change is possible, and it begins with small, intentional actions. This philosophy would later crystallize into the 5 Second Rule, a deceptively simple but profoundly impactful tool that would become the cornerstone of her work.

The journey from legal professional to motivational speaker and author was not without its challenges. Mel faced skepticism, criticism, and moments of self-doubt as she carved out a new identity and career. Yet, she remained steadfast in her commitment to her vision, drawing strength from her experiences and the people she sought to help. She understood that her own struggles and triumphs were not unique but shared by countless others. By embracing her vulnerability and authenticity, she was able to create a sense of connection and trust that transcended cultural and generational boundaries.

Through her work, Mel has redefined the landscape of personal development, challenging traditional notions of success and offering a more inclusive and compassionate perspective. Her journey is a testament to the power of resilience, adaptability, and self-awareness. It is a reminder that even the most challenging experiences can serve as catalysts for growth and transformation. As we continue to explore the chapters of her life, we uncover not just a story of personal reinvention but a blueprint for navigating the complexities of modern life with courage and purpose.

Chapter: 02

The Ripple Effect of Influence

Mel Robbins' story, as it unfolded, was no longer just her own. The seeds of transformation she planted in her own life had grown into a sprawling forest of influence that touched countless lives across the globe. The beauty of her journey lay not only in her personal evolution but also in the way her insights created a domino effect, empowering others to step into their potential. This chapter explores the far-reaching impact of her work, tracing the contours of her influence as it rippled outward, breaking boundaries and reshaping lives.

As Mel's public presence continued to expand, her ideas began to take on a life of their own. The 5 Second Rule became more than just a tool for personal decision-making; it became a universal language of action. People from all walks of life adopted the principle, sharing stories of how it helped them overcome fears, break destructive habits, and pursue long-cherished dreams. From corporate executives making bold moves in their careers to parents reconnecting with their children, the rule transcended demographics and contexts, offering a simple yet profound pathway to change.

The stories of transformation that emerged were as diverse as they were inspiring. A young entrepreneur in Singapore used the 5 Second Rule to pitch a groundbreaking idea that revolutionized his industry. A single mother in Detroit credited it with giving her the courage to return to school and build a better life for her children. A seasoned teacher in rural India found in it the strength to advocate for educational reforms that impacted an entire generation of students. Each story was a testament to the universality of Mel's message and the profound ways it resonated with people across cultures and geographies.

Mel's influence extended beyond the individual to the collective, finding its way into institutions and organizations seeking to foster a culture of growth and innovation. Corporations embraced her principles as tools for enhancing productivity, collaboration, and resilience. Educational institutions incorporated her teachings into their curricula, equipping students with the skills and mindset needed to navigate the challenges of an ever-changing world. Community organizations adopted her frameworks to empower marginalized groups, giving them the confidence to advocate for their rights and pursue opportunities previously deemed out of reach.

Her work also found a natural synergy with the burgeoning field of mental health advocacy. Mel's candid discussions about her own struggles with anxiety and self-doubt resonated deeply with individuals grappling with similar challenges. Her ability to normalize these experiences and provide actionable tools for coping became a beacon of hope for those navigating the often-stigmatized terrain of mental health. Therapists, counselors, and support groups embraced her principles, integrating them into their practices and amplifying their reach. Mel's message served as a reminder that vulnerability and strength are not opposites but two sides of the same coin, and that seeking help is an act of courage, not weakness.

One of the most remarkable aspects of Mel's influence was her ability to foster a sense of community among her audience. Through her social media platforms, online courses, and live events, she created spaces where individuals could connect, share their stories, and celebrate their victories. These communities became sources of inspiration and support, where people from different backgrounds and walks of life came together to learn, grow, and uplift one another. Mel's authenticity and relatability were the glue that held these communities together, making them not just audiences but active participants in a shared journey of transformation.

The ripple effect of Mel's work was not confined to her direct audience; it extended to those influenced by the individuals she inspired. The executive who used the 5 Second Rule to take a bold career leap became a mentor to aspiring leaders, passing on the principles he had learned. The teacher who advocated for educational reforms inspired her students to dream bigger and pursue their ambitions with confidence. The single mother who returned to school became a role model for her children, instilling in them the values of resilience and determination. Each story was a reminder that the impact of one person's courage and growth could create a cascade of positive change, touching lives in ways that could never be fully measured.

As Mel's influence grew, so did her sense of responsibility. She understood that her platform was not just a privilege but a profound opportunity to effect meaningful change. This awareness drove her to continually evolve and refine her message, seeking new ways to connect with her audience and address the challenges they faced. She invested in research and collaboration, partnering with experts and thought leaders to deepen her understanding and expand her impact. Her commitment to integrity and authenticity remained unwavering, guiding her decisions and ensuring that her work remained rooted in genuine care and purpose.

One of the most significant ways Mel sought to expand her impact was through mentorship and advocacy. She recognized the importance of empowering the next generation of leaders, creators, and changemakers, and she dedicated herself to providing them with the tools and support they needed to succeed. Whether through one-on-one mentorship, workshops, or collaborative projects, she poured her energy into nurturing talent and fostering innovation. Her ability to see potential in others and help them unlock it became one of her greatest gifts, leaving a legacy that extended far beyond her own achievements.

Mel's advocacy work also took on new dimensions as she used her platform to amplify voices and causes that aligned with her values. She became a vocal proponent of initiatives aimed at addressing systemic inequalities, promoting mental health awareness, and fostering inclusivity. Her willingness to tackle complex and often uncomfortable issues with empathy and courage earned her respect and admiration, further solidifying her position as a trusted and influential voice. She understood that true leadership required not just speaking out but also listening, learning, and taking action, and she approached her advocacy with the same humility and determination that defined her personal journey.

The ripple effect of Mel's work was perhaps most evident in the countless lives she touched through her books, speeches, and media platforms. The letters, emails, and messages she received from her audience painted a vivid picture of the impact of her words and ideas. They told of lives transformed, relationships healed, dreams pursued, and barriers broken. Each story was a testament to the power of human connection, the resilience of the human spirit, and the profound ways in which one person's courage and authenticity could inspire others to embrace their own.

Through her journey, Mel Robbins has shown that true influence is not about fame or accolades but about the ability to create meaningful, lasting change in the lives of others. Her work is a reminder that every action, no matter how small, has the potential to create a ripple effect, touching lives in ways we may never fully understand. It is a testament to the power of authenticity, courage, and the unwavering belief in the potential for growth and transformation. As we continue to explore her story, we are reminded of the profound interconnectedness of our lives and the extraordinary impact we can have when we choose to lead with purpose and heart.

Chapter: 03

The Power of Reinvention

Mel Robbins' journey into the realm of reinvention was neither planned nor expected; it emerged as an organic response to the hurdles life placed in her path. Reinvention was not merely an act of starting over—it became a profound and ongoing process of rediscovery, one that would allow her to redefine success, reshape her identity, and embrace possibilities she had never dared to dream of. Through her ability to continuously evolve, Mel became a living testament to the idea that reinvention is a cornerstone of human growth and resilience.

Mel's life was a vivid tapestry of transitions, each marked by a blend of personal breakthroughs and seismic shifts in perspective. Her story of reinvention began in moments of discomfort, frustration, and stagnation—places where many people find themselves trapped, uncertain of how to move forward. Yet, for Mel, these moments became catalysts for bold action. She had an uncanny ability to look at what wasn't working, confront it with brutal honesty, and take deliberate steps to chart a new course.

Reinvention began, first and foremost, with the art of letting go. Mel realized that clinging to past roles, identities, and expectations was akin to carrying a heavy load up a steep hill. Whether it was her earlier career as a lawyer, her struggles with financial instability, or the self-imposed limitations she had once placed on herself, she had to unlearn the belief that her past defined her future. This process wasn't easy. Letting go meant facing fears, confronting insecurities, and allowing herself the grace to move beyond the comfort of familiarity.

What set Mel apart in her journey of reinvention was her willingness to embrace experimentation. Instead of viewing change as a daunting and linear process, she saw it as a series of experiments—small, courageous steps that would collectively lead to big transformations. Reinvention, for her, wasn't about having all the answers upfront but about committing to the process of exploration. Whether it was delving into the world of motivational speaking, writing her groundbreaking books, or building a media empire, each new venture was an experiment in its own right, fueled by curiosity and the desire to make a difference.

Her belief in the power of micro-actions played a pivotal role in her reinvention. The 5 Second Rule, which had initially been a personal tool to overcome procrastination and fear, became the backbone of her philosophy on change. With its simplicity and universality, the rule reminded people that massive shifts often begin with small, decisive moments. Mel's own reinvention was a collection of these moments, stitched together by a relentless determination to create a life of purpose and meaning.

The concept of reinvention also extended to the way Mel approached failure. Instead of viewing setbacks as dead ends, she reframed them as learning opportunities—valuable data points that informed her next move. Her candor about her failures resonated deeply with audiences, offering a refreshing perspective on the often romanticized narratives of success. Mel's ability to turn her missteps into stepping stones demonstrated a rare resilience, inspiring others to see failure not as a reflection of their worth but as a natural part of the journey toward reinvention.

As Mel ventured into the world of public speaking and writing, her capacity for reinvention became evident in the way she connected with her audience. She wasn't interested in presenting a polished, unattainable version of herself; instead, she embraced vulnerability as a superpower. By sharing her struggles and triumphs with unfiltered honesty, she invited others to see their own potential for growth. Reinvention, as she showed, was not about perfection—it was about progress, about being brave enough to start over and humble enough to keep learning.

The ripple effect of Mel's reinvention was profound. It wasn't just her life that transformed; her story ignited a spark in others to take control of their own narratives. Her message resonated with people across the spectrum—those at the beginning of their journeys, those in the midst of upheaval, and even those who had achieved success but were yearning for something more. Mel became a beacon for anyone who had ever felt stuck, offering not just hope but practical tools to begin anew.

Her ability to reinvent herself also influenced the way she navigated her personal relationships. As her sense of self evolved, so too did her capacity to connect with others on a deeper level. She approached her relationships with the same principles she applied to her work: authenticity, intentionality, and the courage to address what wasn't working. Reinvention, as Mel demonstrated, was not a solitary pursuit—it was intertwined with the people and communities around her, creating a dynamic interplay of growth and connection.

Perhaps one of the most remarkable aspects of Mel's reinvention was her ability to remain grounded amid the whirlwind of change. Despite her growing fame and influence, she stayed true to her core values, using her platform to amplify messages of empowerment and inclusivity. Her authenticity was her anchor, allowing her to navigate the complexities of reinvention without losing sight of who she was and what she stood for.

The power of reinvention, as embodied by Mel Robbins, lies in its infinite possibilities. It is a process that invites us to shed old skin, embrace the unknown, and continuously redefine what it means to live a fulfilled life. Mel's journey serves as a reminder that reinvention is not reserved for the fortunate few—it is a choice available to anyone willing to confront their fears, take action, and trust in the unfolding of their path. Her story is a celebration of the human spirit's capacity to adapt, evolve, and create anew, offering a timeless message of hope and empowerment to all who encounter it.

Chapter: 04

Empowering the Masses Through Actionable Wisdom

Mel Robbins' journey to becoming a global icon of empowerment was not one marked by grandiose promises or abstract philosophies. Instead, it was rooted in an unrelenting commitment to providing people with tools they could use immediately to improve their lives. Actionable wisdom became her hallmark, a guiding force that turned her into a trusted voice for millions who yearned for practical solutions in a world often saturated with empty rhetoric.

Her approach was refreshingly pragmatic. Mel had no patience for overly complex strategies that felt disconnected from the struggles of everyday people. She understood that the barriers to change were not merely external but deeply internal. Fear, procrastination, and self-doubt were the silent saboteurs that kept people stuck, and Mel's mission was to dismantle these barriers with tools that were as simple as they were transformative.

The cornerstone of her philosophy, the 5 Second Rule, was emblematic of this approach. With its origins rooted in a single moment of personal struggle, the rule evolved into a universal framework for overcoming hesitation and taking immediate action. It wasn't just a strategy; it was a movement, one that resonated across cultures, languages, and socioeconomic boundaries. The simplicity of counting backward from five to one before taking action belied its profound psychological impact. By interrupting patterns of doubt and hesitation, the 5 Second Rule gave people a tangible way to reclaim control over their decisions.

What set Mel apart was her ability to bridge the gap between science and accessibility. She delved into the neuroscience behind the 5 Second Rule, explaining how the prefrontal cortex could be activated to disrupt autopilot behaviors and initiate purposeful action. Yet, she presented this information in a way that was relatable and easy to grasp. Her explanations weren't buried in academic jargon; they were enlivened by anecdotes, humor, and a deep understanding of the human experience. Mel's ability to connect complex concepts to real-life applications was a testament to her genius as a communicator.

Her teachings went beyond the rule itself. Mel had an innate ability to identify the hidden patterns that governed people's lives, from the way they talked to themselves to the stories they told about their own limitations. She challenged her audience to rewrite those narratives, to see themselves not as victims of circumstance but as architects of their futures. This wasn't about blind optimism; it was about cultivating a mindset of agency and accountability.

Mel's influence extended far beyond her books and speeches. Her digital presence became a lifeline for those seeking daily inspiration. Whether it was through her social media posts, podcasts, or live broadcasts, she offered a steady stream of wisdom that was as raw as it was uplifting. Her willingness to share her own struggles—from financial hardship to marital challenges—created an authenticity that made her teachings all the more powerful. People saw themselves in her story, and this connection turned followers into loyal advocates of her message.

The resonance of Mel's work was evident in the countless testimonials she received from people whose lives had been transformed. From the single mother who used the 5 Second Rule to return to school and earn her degree, to the entrepreneur who overcame paralyzing fear to launch a successful business, Mel's impact was both profound and deeply personal. These stories were not just testaments to her methods; they were a reflection of her unwavering belief in the potential of the human spirit.

One of the most remarkable aspects of Mel's approach was her emphasis on small actions leading to big changes. She understood that transformation rarely happened in sweeping gestures but in the cumulative effect of consistent, intentional choices. This perspective was liberating for her audience, many of whom felt overwhelmed by the idea of change. Mel's message was clear: you don't need to have it all figured out to move forward. All it takes is one small step—and then another.

Her ability to inspire action was amplified by her unique style of delivery. Mel's energy was infectious, her passion palpable. Whether she was speaking on stage, appearing on a morning show, or recording a podcast, she brought an intensity that made people sit up and listen. Yet, beneath the dynamism was a profound sense of empathy. Mel's success as a motivator lay in her ability to see people—to understand their fears, dreams, and frustrations—and to speak to those truths with compassion and clarity.

Mel's focus on empowerment extended to every aspect of her work. She wasn't interested in creating a dependency on her methods; her goal was to equip people with tools they could use independently. This philosophy was evident in the way she structured her teachings, always emphasizing personal responsibility and self-reliance. Mel wanted her audience to feel not just inspired but capable, to walk away with the confidence that they could create change on their own terms.

As her influence grew, so did her commitment to expanding the reach of her message. Mel's ventures into new platforms and mediums were driven by a desire to meet people where they were. From online courses to interactive workshops, she continuously innovated to ensure that her teachings were accessible to as many people as possible. Her ability to adapt to the changing landscape of media while staying true to her core values was a testament to her versatility and vision.

Mel's work was not without its challenges. As her platform grew, so did the scrutiny. Critics questioned the simplicity of her methods, suggesting that real change required more than a five-second decision. But Mel welcomed these conversations, viewing them as an opportunity to deepen the dialogue about personal growth. She was the first to acknowledge that the 5 Second Rule was not a magic bullet but a starting point—a tool that, when combined with effort and commitment, could lead to extraordinary results.

The impact of Mel's actionable wisdom extended beyond individuals to communities and organizations. Her teachings became a staple in workplaces, where leaders used her principles to foster productivity, collaboration, and innovation. By addressing the human element of professional success, Mel brought a new dimension to the conversation about workplace dynamics. Her insights into motivation, focus, and resilience resonated with employees and executives alike, creating a ripple effect of empowerment across industries.

As Mel's influence continued to grow, she remained deeply connected to her purpose. For her, the work was never about fame or accolades; it was about making a difference. She saw herself not as a guru but as a guide, someone who could illuminate a path forward for those willing to take the first step. This humility, combined with her unwavering dedication, made her a beacon of hope for millions around the world.

Empowering the masses through actionable wisdom was more than a mission for Mel Robbins; it was her legacy. Through her teachings, she showed that the power to change lies within each of us, waiting to be unlocked by a single moment of courage. Her story is a testament to the transformative power of small actions, the resilience of the human spirit, and the boundless potential that comes from believing in oneself.

Chapter: 05

Embracing the Future with Confidence and Courage

As the luminous arc of Mel Robbins' journey continued to evolve, it became clear that her influence had not merely been a passing phenomenon but an enduring force of transformation. The foundation of her early struggles and her steadfast resolve had shaped an individual whose ability to inspire transcended barriers of age, geography, and personal circumstance. By this juncture, Mel had woven herself into the fabric of modern self-help and empowerment, her voice echoing in countless lives that sought solace and renewal in her words.

The trajectory of Mel's work carried her to uncharted territories where the essence of her philosophy was tested against ever-changing societal backdrops. She had always been deeply attuned to the human condition—the silent fears that paralyzed, the unchecked anxieties that suffocated dreams, and the hidden strengths waiting to be uncovered. But as the world evolved—with the advent of rapidly advancing technology, shifting social norms, and emerging global crises—so too did the challenges faced by individuals. And Mel, ever adaptable, rose to meet them with unmatched clarity and courage.

In the throes of the digital revolution, Mel discovered fertile ground to further her mission. Social media platforms, once dismissed as superficial and transient, became her pulpit—spaces where she cultivated authentic relationships with a sprawling audience. Her approach, as always, was deeply human. Mel understood the allure of instant gratification but also the deep yearning for connection and meaning that lay beneath the digital facade. Rather than succumbing to the impersonal nature of technology, she humanized it, forging bonds that felt personal despite the virtual chasm. Her videos, often unscripted and raw, captured the essence of her authenticity. Each clip, whether two minutes or twenty, carried the same unwavering message: that change, though daunting, was within reach.

The response was staggering. Mel's audience grew exponentially, comprising individuals from every walk of life. Teenagers grappling with self-doubt, professionals teetering on the brink of burnout, parents navigating the challenges of modern parenting—all found a lifeline in her words. Yet, what set her apart from countless others offering advice in the digital sphere was her uncanny ability to make each person feel seen and heard. It wasn't merely the content of her message but the conviction with which she delivered it. Mel's relatability wasn't manufactured; it was a natural extension of her genuine empathy and her unrelenting commitment to serve.

As her digital presence expanded, so too did the scope of her work. The Five-Second Rule, her cornerstone concept, continued to evolve in relevance. It was no longer confined to personal decision-making or overcoming procrastination; it became a tool for navigating the complexities of a hyperconnected world. Mel began exploring its applications in team dynamics, leadership strategies, and even the realm of mental health. Workshops and seminars, once intimate gatherings, now drew thousands, each attendee eager to glean insights that would catalyze their own transformation.

Her writing, too, underwent a renaissance. While her earlier works had focused on individual empowerment, her later books delved into collective resilience and the power of community. She examined how societal shifts—from the global pandemic to movements for social justice—had reshaped the way people connected and collaborated. Mel's prose, as always, was a reflection of her character—bold, insightful, and deeply personal. She didn't shy away from addressing polarizing topics or sharing her own vulnerabilities, recognizing that true growth often emerged from discomfort and confrontation.

The stage remained a central pillar of Mel's life. Despite her success in other mediums, she never lost her love for live speaking. There was something uniquely electric about the energy of a crowd, the palpable connection that arose when she shared her story in real-time. Each event, whether in a packed arena or an intimate conference hall, was an opportunity for Mel to reinforce the universality of her message. She thrived in these spaces, her charisma and authenticity creating a resonance that lingered long after the final applause.

Amid her professional endeavors, Mel's personal life continued to be a wellspring of inspiration. Her family remained her anchor, a source of strength and a reminder of the values that had guided her from the outset. Her relationship with her children—once a tender dynamic shaped by her own struggles with self-worth—had blossomed into one of mutual respect and admiration. As they navigated their own paths, Mel's influence was evident in their courage and resilience, a testament to her impact not just as a public figure but as a mother.

Mel's marriage, too, was a reflection of her growth. It had weathered its share of challenges, moments when doubt and disconnection threatened to overshadow the love that had brought them together. But just as Mel had transformed her relationship with herself, she brought the same intentionality to her partnership. She and her husband, united by a shared commitment to growth, approached their bond as a living entity—one that required nurturing, understanding, and occasional reinvention. Their journey wasn't without its imperfections, but it was marked by a profound sense of purpose and unity.

As Mel's reach extended across continents, her impact transcended the boundaries of language and culture. Translators and interpreters worked tirelessly to adapt her work for diverse audiences, ensuring that her message retained its essence in every tongue. Mel herself took an active role in these endeavors, collaborating with cultural experts to ensure that her concepts resonated universally. She understood that empowerment wasn't a one-size-fits-all solution; it required sensitivity to the unique contexts and challenges faced by individuals around the globe.

Philanthropy became an increasingly significant aspect of Mel's life. While she had always been passionate about giving back, her success afforded her the means to create lasting change on a broader scale. She established initiatives aimed at supporting mental health awareness, providing educational resources for underserved communities, and fostering leadership among marginalized groups. Mel's approach to philanthropy was as hands-on as her other endeavors. She didn't merely write checks; she immersed herself in the work, partnering with grassroots organizations and amplifying the voices of those she sought to help.

Through it all, Mel remained acutely aware of the delicate balance between her public and private selves. Fame, with all its trappings, had never been her goal. She viewed her platform not as a pedestal but as a bridge—a means of connecting with others and amplifying their own potential. Her humility, rare in an era often characterized by self-promotion, endeared her to those who followed her journey. She never lost sight of the fact that her success was inextricably linked to the trust and faith placed in her by countless individuals. It was a responsibility she bore with grace and gratitude.

The future, as Mel often reminded her audience, was unwritten. She embraced it with the same courage and curiosity that had defined her journey thus far. Challenges would undoubtedly arise, as they always did, but Mel faced them with a quiet confidence born of experience. She had weathered storms and emerged stronger, not in spite of them but because of them. And as she looked ahead, she did so with an unwavering belief in the transformative power of hope, action, and connection.

Mel Robbins' story was far from over. It was a testament to the boundless potential of the human spirit, a narrative shaped by courage, resilience, and an unyielding commitment to growth. As her journey continued to unfold, one thing was certain: her legacy would endure, a beacon of possibility for generations to come.

Chapter: 06

Becoming a Global Voice for Change

To step into the world of global impact requires a boldness that defies the mundane and an audacity to challenge the entrenched. As Mel Robbins found herself entering the next epoch of her life, she was no longer simply the woman who had created the groundbreaking 5 Second Rule. She had become a voice of global resonance—an undeniable force whose influence spanned continents, industries, and generations. Her journey was not merely about success or fame; it was about the power of transformation—individual and collective—and the profound ways in which her words, her presence, and her relentless dedication to authenticity could shape a more conscious, resilient world.

The first indicators of this global reach began subtly, as whispers of her influence reached audiences she never imagined she could touch. Her talks, already viral, were being translated into multiple languages, spreading to cultures and communities that saw her message as a lifeline. The universality of her ideas became a testament to her ability to distill complex emotions into actionable wisdom. People from vastly different walks of life—a farmer in rural India, a young entrepreneur in South Korea, a grandmother in Brazil—found themselves drawn to her honesty, her practicality, and her unapologetic embrace of the human experience. These moments, seemingly small and scattered, began to form the threads of a tapestry that would define Mel's global legacy.

As invitations from international stages began to pour in, Mel found herself traversing the globe—from the buzzing streets of Tokyo to the historic halls of Oxford University. Each speech carried the weight of responsibility, a deep awareness that her words could ripple outward to shift perspectives and ignite movements. In Tokyo, she spoke to a generation of workers struggling with burnout, bringing a sense of renewal to a culture steeped in relentless dedication.

In Johannesburg, she addressed young women aspiring to break barriers, sharing her own stories of overcoming doubt and societal expectations. Every destination held its unique challenges, but Mel's message transcended borders, resonating with the shared humanity that underpins all of us.

What set Mel apart in these moments was her unwavering commitment to authenticity. Unlike many who adapt their message to fit cultural norms or expectations, she brought her unfiltered self to every stage. She shared her failures as openly as her triumphs, her insecurities alongside her confidence. This vulnerability became her superpower, forging connections that were as profound as they were unexpected. In an era increasingly dominated by curated perfection, Mel's rawness was a breath of fresh air—a reminder that imperfection is not a weakness but a fundamental part of what makes us human.

Beyond her public speaking, Mel's global influence was further amplified by her ventures into new forms of media. Her podcast, which began as a small, personal project, exploded in popularity, reaching millions of listeners around the world. Each episode was a masterclass in storytelling and practical wisdom, blending her signature humor and candor with deep, often transformative insights. Whether interviewing world leaders, artists, or everyday individuals with extraordinary stories, Mel created a space where vulnerability and inspiration coexisted. The podcast became more than just a platform; it was a movement, a gathering place for those seeking to better understand themselves and the world around them.

Social media, too, became an essential tool in her arsenal. Mel's posts were not the polished, carefully curated content typical of influencers; they were raw, real, and deeply personal. A video of her struggling through a particularly hard day, or a post about a moment of doubt, would often go viral, not because they were glamorous, but because they were relatable. Her willingness to share the messy, unfiltered parts of her life made her a beacon for authenticity in a digital age increasingly defined by artifice. These platforms allowed her to interact directly with her audience, creating a sense of intimacy that few public figures could achieve.

As her global influence grew, so too did her sense of responsibility. Mel began to use her platform to advocate for causes close to her heart. Mental health, always a cornerstone of her work, became an even greater focus. She partnered with organizations around the world to destigmatize conversations around anxiety, depression, and stress. Her campaigns were not just about raising awareness but about providing tangible tools and resources. In schools, workplaces, and communities, her initiatives brought meaningful change, breaking down barriers and empowering individuals to take control of their mental well-being.

But her advocacy did not stop there. Mel also became a fierce champion for women's rights, diversity, and inclusion. Her own experiences—as a woman in media, as a mother, as someone who had faced and overcome systemic biases—fueled her passion for these issues. She worked tirelessly to amplify marginalized voices, using her influence to shine a light on stories that might otherwise go unheard. Whether mentoring young female entrepreneurs or speaking out against inequality on global platforms, Mel's commitment to justice was unwavering. She understood that true leadership is not about standing above others but about lifting them up, and she lived that principle every day.

As she expanded her reach, Mel also faced new challenges. The demands of a global presence took a toll, forcing her to confront the delicate balance between ambition and well-being. She spoke openly about these struggles, turning them into opportunities for growth and learning. Her transparency about the pressures of success resonated deeply with her audience, many of whom faced similar challenges in their own lives. Through her example, she showed that it is possible to pursue greatness without sacrificing one's humanity.

Perhaps one of the most remarkable aspects of Mel's global journey was her ability to remain grounded. Despite her fame and influence, she never lost sight of what truly mattered. Her family remained her anchor, a source of love and support that kept her rooted in the midst of her whirlwind life. She often spoke about the importance of gratitude, taking time each day to reflect on the blessings in her life. This practice, simple yet profound, became a central theme in her teachings, inspiring countless others to cultivate their own sense of gratitude.

Mel's global influence was not just about the scope of her reach but the depth of her impact. She did not seek to be a celebrity or an icon; she sought to be a catalyst for change. Her work was not about her but about the millions of lives she touched, the hearts she opened, the minds she expanded. She believed deeply in the power of individuals to create ripples of change, and she dedicated her life to empowering others to do just that.

As Mel looked back on this phase of her journey, she saw not a series of achievements but a collection of connections—moments where her words, her actions, and her presence had made a difference. These moments, small and large, were the true measure of her success. They were the legacy she hoped to leave behind: a world slightly kinder, slightly braver, slightly more authentic because she had dared to be herself and encouraged others to do the same.

In the end, Mel Robbins' global voice was not about volume but about resonance. It was not about speaking to the world but about listening to it, understanding it, and responding with compassion, wisdom, and courage. It was a voice that echoed in boardrooms and classrooms, in homes and hearts, in the quiet moments of doubt and the triumphant moments of discovery. It was a voice that reminded us all of our potential—not just to achieve but to connect, to grow, and to transform. And it was a voice that, long after her time, would continue to inspire generations to come.

Conclusion

Mel Robbins' impact on the world transcends the simple act of motivating people; it's a living, breathing testament to the transformative power of action. Over the years, she has meticulously crafted a legacy that embodies the very essence of change. Her journey, which began in moments of deep personal struggle and self-doubt, has evolved into a beacon of empowerment for millions. Her work, which initially began as a series of personal breakthroughs, has now become a global movement.

The 5 Second Rule, a concept that emerged from a moment of personal desperation, has become a lifeline for countless individuals. It's not just a tool for self-improvement; it's a cultural shift. Mel's teaching isn't about grandiose speeches or abstract theories. It's about small, actionable steps that change lives, and this simplicity is precisely what makes her methods so powerful. Her unique approach to transformation isn't rooted in complexity, but in the art of simplifying the path to change.

Her influence on modern self-help culture is nothing short of revolutionary. In a world flooded with endless advice and contradictory philosophies, Mel Robbins stands as a figure who brings clarity to the noise. She doesn't promise miracle cures or instant fixes. Instead, she offers something more profound: the ability to take control of one's own life through intentional action. This no-nonsense approach is what has made her a figure of such remarkable authenticity. Her reliability resonates with people from all walks of life, not because of her success, but because of the very human struggles she openly shares with her audience. She doesn't present herself as a perfect example of triumph, but as someone who has faced her own failures, fears, and moments of despair—and emerged stronger. This human touch, grounded in vulnerability, has formed the bedrock of her legacy.

Mel's success is not just the story of an individual; it's a collective story, shared by the millions who have applied her principles and experienced change. Whether it's a person overcoming procrastination, a mother reclaiming her confidence, or a young professional taking the first steps towards their dreams, Mel Robbins has empowered individuals to act, to push past their doubts, and to create their own momentum. Her message has permeated classrooms, boardrooms, living rooms, and beyond. It's not just about personal development; it's about the power to influence one's environment and the world around them.

What sets Mel apart is her ability to connect deeply with people, to see them, hear them, and inspire them to take action. Her words aren't just motivational fluff; they're calls to action that have inspired real, lasting change. She doesn't just give advice—she gives people permission to take ownership of their lives, to make mistakes, and to grow from them. Her message isn't about perfection; it's about progress. It's about showing up every day, even when the path seems uncertain, and choosing to take action regardless of fear.

As a writer and speaker, Mel's unique ability to speak directly to her audience is one of the cornerstones of her lasting influence. Her books, including *The 5 Second Rule* and *Stop Saying You're Fine*, have become staples in the self-help genre. Yet, what truly sets them apart is their practical applicability. Her writing isn't academic or theoretical—it's down-to-earth, grounded in real-life experiences. It's a reflection of her journey, as well as the struggles of countless others. Through her words, she has made self-help accessible to people who might have previously dismissed it as another abstract, unattainable ideal.

Her TEDx talk, which has garnered millions of views, is a prime example of the power of her message. The simplicity of her idea—counting down from five to silence the inner critic—strikes a chord because it's something everyone can relate to. It's an idea so simple, yet so profound, that it feels like a secret she's sharing with the world. She doesn't just talk about change—she makes it possible for people to experience it in real-time. She's not asking her audience to aspire to some far-off dream; she's teaching them to take the first step, right now.

The 5 Second Rule, which has become her signature concept, is far more than just a personal productivity hack. It's a way of living—an approach to life that encourages people to seize the moment, take action, and silence the voice of hesitation that holds them back. Through this simple principle, Mel has given individuals the power to break free from the cycle of procrastination and self-doubt. She has shown them that the smallest action, when done consistently, can lead to monumental changes.

As her influence continues to grow, it's clear that Mel Robbins is not just a temporary figure in the self-help world. Her impact is long-lasting, and her legacy is one of profound change and empowerment. She is not merely a trendsetter or a passing figure; she is a pioneer who has redefined what it means to take control of one's life. Her contributions go beyond the realm of self-help; they have become a cultural phenomenon. The 5 Second Rule has transcended the confines of personal development and is now part of a broader conversation about how we live our lives, how we confront our fears, and how we make decisions that align with our deepest values.

Looking to the future, Mel Robbins shows no signs of slowing down. Her next projects are already stirring anticipation among her followers. Whether it's new books, speaking engagements, or collaborations, her influence is only poised to grow. She has already written the blueprint for how individuals can transform their lives through action, but her work is far from finished. The world is changing, and Mel Robbins is right there, leading the charge, ready to inspire the next generation of individuals to embrace their power and step into their potential.

Her legacy will not be defined solely by the books she has written, the talks she has given, or the advice she has shared. It will be defined by the countless lives she has touched—the people who, because of her, have found the courage to take the first step, to act despite fear, and to create the life they desire. Mel Robbins has not just empowered a generation; she has created a ripple effect that will continue for years to come. Through her message, she has shown that the key to transformation is not some far-off ideal; it's in the choices we make, every single day.

As she looks ahead, the future holds limitless possibilities. Mel Robbins is not just an author, speaker, or coach; she is a catalyst for change, an architect of action, and a visionary who understands that true empowerment lies in the ability to act—now, without hesitation. Her legacy will continue to inspire generations to come, urging them to take action, to believe in themselves, and to live a life of purpose.

MEL ROBBINS

Let Them Theory Book

Pioneering Personal Development for Generations to Come

Charley C. Goff

www.ingramcontent.com/pod-product-compliance
Lightning Source LLC
LaVergne TN
LVHW050324280125
802302LV00005B/729